ICT

D0121341

THE NEW BASIC SKILL

ICT The New Basic Skill

Leicester: NIACE, 2003   1862011214

ICT

THE NEW BASIC SKILL

ALAN CLARKE
and
LISA ENGLEBRIGHT

niace
promoting adult learning

niace
promoting adult learning

Published by the
National Institute of Adult Continuing Education
(England and Wales)
Renaissance House
20 Princess Road West
Leicester LE1 6TP
Company registration no: 2603322
Charity registration no: 1002775

NIACE has a broad remit to promote lifelong learning opportunities for adults. NIACE works to develop increased participation in education and training, particularly for those who do not have easy access because of barriers of class, gender, age, race, language and culture, learning difficulties and disabilities, or insufficient financial resources.

First published 2003

For a full catalogue of NIACE's publications, please visit
http://www.niace.org.uk/publications

Cataloguing in Publications Data
A CIP record for this title is available from the British Library

ISBN 1 86201 121 4

All photographs courtesy of Nick Hayes
Cover design by Hobo Design Associates, Leicester
Designed and typeset by Creative, Oxford
Printed and bound in Great Britain by Alden Group Limited, Oxford

Contents

Acknowledgements

We would like to thank our colleagues at NIACE for their support and assistance, in particular Peter Lavender and the Information and ICT Learning teams.

Introduction

Information and Communication Technology (ICT) has already made significant changes to the way we work, learn, relax and govern ourselves. These changes are continuing and accelerating. It is rapidly becoming a necessity to use ICT in order to gain and retain employment, have access to government information and to take advantage of new learning opportunities. Many people regard ICT as being critical to competitive advantage. Almost every educational institution is considering how to use technology to support and deliver learning. Television, radio and newspapers now have an online presence. Even a visit to an art gallery or museum can now involve being offered the opportunity to view other items or learn more about the exhibitions through technology. If you are seeking to purchase a kitchen you will often be offered the chance to design your ideal one on a computer. This is now so natural that we have all come to expect it.

For several years people have speculated that ICT is now a basic skill in the same way that reading, writing and using numbers are. In July 2003, the Government's Skill Strategy announced that ICT would be a new skill for life, or basic skill (Department for Education and Skills, 2003a). This publication examines the impact that ICT skills have on individuals and considers if this is comparable to other skills for life.

The OECD (2002), commenting on the way international governments viewed ICT skills, stated that:

> *ICT Skills have become a new type of "general" skill, like literacy or numeracy.*

The e-Learning Task Force (2002) reported that

> *...it is clear that a lack of ICT skills, including not having the skills to learn through ICT, is potentially as great a barrier to employability and social inclusion as a lack of achievement in literacy and numeracy...*

The DELG (2002) report states that

> *...these new competences are fast taking on the characteristics of essential or core skills for the twenty-first century, increasingly on a par with basic literacy and numeracy.*

The DfES's Cybrarian project (Department for Education and Skills, 2002) estimated that there could be approximately 24 million people who are unable to use the Internet. Many of these people are socially or economically disadvantaged. The scale of the problem is huge and greater in scale than that of poor basic literacy and numeracy skills (7 million people).

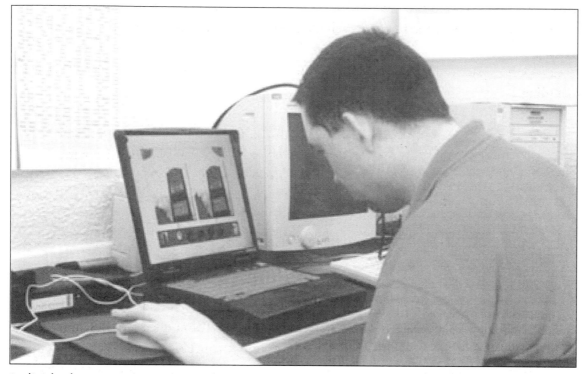

Individual computer user

What is the impact of poor basic skills?

A person who has poor basic skills is likely to face many barriers and disadvantages in their lives. They often earn less than others, are more frequently unemployed and find it difficult to obtain employment. They are limited in the support they can provide their children; are vulnerable in a form-filling culture; have fewer educational opportunities; and often feel stigmatised (OECD, 1997; Moser, 1999). These are significant disadvantages and can lead to their being excluded from elements of society. Does a lack of ICT skills have a similar impact on a person's life?

One major difference between ICT and other basic skills is that in order to become an ICT user the ability to read and write is required and, in the case of spreadsheets and similar applications, a user also needs to be numerate. The level of basic skills required depends on the context in which you are working. The minimum levels of literacy and numeracy required to learn to use ICT are difficult to define precisely. However, it is likely that they will include:

- Some specialist vocabulary (e.g. windows, icons, mouse, pointer, etc.).
- Understanding the visual language of a graphical user interface (GUI).
- Recognising specialist navigation functions (e.g. menus, hyperlinks and scroll bars).
- Keyboard and mouse skills.

This is a substantial requirement which is partially relieved by the assistance some applications provide in the form of spell checkers, thesauruses and predictive lexicons.

What is the impact of limited literacy and numeracy skills? There are a variety of effects including:

1. *Income.* This can be considered in terms of the advantage of literacy or the disadvantage of poor basic skills. Research indicates that incomes rise with educational attainment, while a lack of literacy and numeracy skills is associated with significantly lower incomes (OECD, 1997). The Moser report (Moser, 1999) concludes that poor basic skills are frequently linked to low incomes. This is more closely related to numeracy and is apparent across a range of countries (e.g. Canada, United Kingdom and Australia).

2. *Employment.* The Moser report (Moser, 1999) states that adults with poor basic skills are five times more likely to be unemployed. For employed adults poor literacy or numeracy skills will clearly limit opportunities and almost certainly reduce career progression. Modern training practice places an emphasis on the use of learning materials that require good literacy skills so that adults with poor skills are at a disadvantage.

3. *Economy.* Poor basic skills often mean people are restricted to taking low-paid jobs with little chance of progression. Additionally, the impact of poor basic skills on the UK economy is estimated to cost business and government £10 billion a year (Ernst and Young in Moser, 1999).

4. *Health.* OECD (1997) reports that there is a relationship between good health and literacy. The Moser report (Moser, 1999) identifies that adults with poor basic skills are more likely to have poor health. A key reason suggested by the OECD is that literate adults are able to locate and understand information about health issues. An alternative view is that poverty is linked to poor education and health.

5. *Children.* Children who have parents with poor literacy and numeracy skills are also likely to have difficulties with reading, writing and number (Moser, 1999). However, this may not simply be due to their parents' poor skills although they will probably be limited in the help they can provide their children.

6. *Participation.* To take part in many aspects of society requires participants who have good literacy and numeracy skills. To make informed decisions requires adults who are able to locate information and interpret it. This clearly will be limited if the adult has poor basic skills.

7. *Society.* The National Strategy (2001) states that poor literacy and numeracy skills have "disasterous consequences for the individuals concerned, weakens the country's ability to compete in the global economy and places a huge burden on society".

8. *Stigma.* Anecdotal evidence strongly suggests that many adults with poor literacy and numeracy skills are unwilling to admit they have a problem due to a fear of being stigmatised.

9. *Education.* Bynner (2001) gives an overview of the factors which may improve with education such as health, crime, citizenship and family life. Poor literacy and numeracy will limit the educational opportunities of which a person will be able to take advantage.

10. *Confidence.* Adults with poor basic skills may lack confidence in their ability to participate fully in society while they are unable to make sense of, or edit and shape, the written word that controls it.

The impact of poor literacy and numeracy skills is clearly significant to both the individuals concerned and society. Does a lack of ICT skills produce a similar level of difficulty?

What is basic ICT?

In order to consider ICT as a new basic skill it is important to be sure that it is clearly defined. However, this presents a problem in that it is a general term that is widely used to include many different technologies. One approach is to consider what the term 'Information Communication Technology' includes:

- Computer systems (e.g. manipulating and saving files).
- Computer applications (e.g. word processing, spreadsheets and databases).
- Communication technologies (e.g. e-mail, mobile telephones and using the Internet).
- Using home and community technologies (e.g. using an Automated Telling Machine, video recorder, DVD player and digital cameras).
- Computer hardware (e.g. printers, scanners and digital equipment).

ICT includes computer, domestic and commercial systems and equipment. It covers the use of technology to handle information and aid communication. However, there are other related terms which may form part of the argument for ICT to become a basic skill. Information and Learning Technology (ILT) is concerned with the use of ICT to deliver and support learning. Without ICT skills learners will to some extent be excluded from the benefits of ILT. E-learning forms part of the definition of ILT which requires specific technical and learning skills to take part.

Several awarding bodies have defined various levels of ICT skills, knowledge and understanding. These definitions are often in the context of employment and education (OCR, 2002a,b). They are approved by the Qualifications and Curriculum Authority, so provide a means of defining ICT skills, and could be compared to the definitions of literacy and numeracy skills.

New CLAIT is probably the most widely available and used level 1 ICT qualification. It includes both mandatory and optional units. The mandatory unit covers the use of computers and the management of information while there are nine optional units including word processing, electronic communications, spreadsheets, databases, desktop publishing, graphs and charts, computer art, web page creation, and presentation graphics (Clarke, 2002c). Even with this impressive range of optional units New CLAIT does not cover all the possible technologies within ICT or directly those required for ILT or e-learning. A definition of basic ICT skills would need to consider the inclusion of these types of skill.

A significant characteristic of ICT is that it is continually changing and developing. New versions of existing applications are regularly released while new products are constantly being developed. This has an important impact on ICT skills in that users must be able to adapt to new products and versions of existing applications. This requires them to both transfer their existing knowledge and skills and be able to learn new ones, in many cases independently. In order to successfully adapt to new products users are required to develop a structural understanding of ICT applications, systems and hardware. This will allow them to adjust to change naturally and effectively. This structural understanding must be included in any definition of ICT – the basic skill.

At the moment it is doubtful whether a sufficient degree of structural understanding is developed by many ICT courses, which tend to focus on developing a functional understanding/competence of applications. Equally important is that to transfer learning to new situations requires confidence. Many people who can competently use an application have insufficient confidence to learn to use a related application without support. Also, ICT is always launching new products and processes which need to be understood. It is therefore likely that lifelong learning applies more to ICT skills and understanding than many other subjects.

The way ICT is deployed varies depending on the situation in which it is being used. A definition based on employment may emphasise finding information and entering information databases (e.g. call centre staff), while one focused on e-learning will include the use of e-mail to communicate to peers and tutors. Alternatively, one that considers citizenship may concentrate on the Internet (e.g. searching for information, taking part in online forums and judging the quality of online data). There is a need to consider the priorities of different needs and aspirations in any definition. The current level 1 qualifications are probably mostly aimed at employment, although the inclusion of units on subjects such as computer art shows a wider perspective. A simple consideration of job advertisements shows that the emphasis is often placed on the ability to use a particular application, that is, on the functional understanding of a product. However, we have already seen that to cope with change requires a more structural understanding, while a great deal of ICT also requires generic skills such as searching, assessing and adapting information. The ability to transfer prior learning is an important characteristic of being a competent ICT user.

A definition of basic ICT will need to include:

- functional knowledge;
- structural understanding; and
- generic skills (including transfer of learning)

in the context of a wide range of hardware and software applications and systems. The other factor is that ICT technology changes continuously and any definition will need to be regularly reviewed. In addition, the impact of ICT on work practices is also likely to change. Many e-mail users rapidly discover that the volume of messages quickly overwhelms them unless they change their working practices to cope with it. A common tactic is to file messages in a number of folders and many users employ complex structures of nested folders. However, research has shown that a simple flat structure is best practice (Ducheneaut and Bellotti, 2001). This illustrates that simple functional skills are not sufficient to become an effective user of ICT. E-mail, in a similar way to many other applications, is often employed for far more than simple messaging. Mackay (1998) showed that e-mail was used for task and time management in addition to communication.

This section has considered what the nature of basic ICT is in a technical sense. However, we should not forget the consequences of a lack of ICT skills and understanding. These are likely to be:

- Reduced opportunities to find and sustain employment.
- Reduced access to local and national public information and thus fewer chances to make informed decisions.

- Less opportunity to take advantage of online shopping and thus to gain more value for money.
- Inability to support children's learning.
- Reduced channels of communication.

These points can be summarised as people being disadvantaged both economically and socially. Later sections will consider these issues in more depth.

Key points

1. ICT has and is continuing to make significant changes in all aspects of people's lives.
2. ICT has been designated a skill for life.
3. There are approximately 24 million people without ICT skills compared to 7 million with poor literacy and numeracy skills.
4. People with poor literacy and numeracy skills face many barriers and disadvantages in their lives (e.g. lower incomes and periods of unemployment).
5. The definition of basic ICT is likely to include a mixture of functional, structural and generic skills in the context of hardware and software.

Current position

Fifty-six per cent of the adult population of Great Britain accessed the Internet during the period from October to December 2001 (National Statistics, 2002). Thirty-nine per cent of households have access to the Internet. Access is mainly through the use of personal computers but the survey includes all forms of access (e.g. digital television). However, 98 per cent of households access the Internet through personal computers. The survey has consistently shown a growth in the number of households gaining access to the Internet during the last three years, although some observers of the use of ICT anticipate that the growth will begin to slow or even to stabilise.

These headline figures tend to disguise a more complex picture of access. Men and women now use the Internet almost equally following a rapid increase in the number of women accessing the Internet while the proportion of men has remained relatively stable. In February 2002, 58 per cent of men and 54 per cent of women used the Internet. However, this image of equality does not extend to the age of the user with a large majority of 16 to 24-year-olds using the Internet (i.e. 80 per cent) compared to a small minority of adults aged 65 and over (i.e. 12 per cent) (National Statistics, 2002). Similar differences are also apparent if the income of the adults is considered. People on the lowest incomes have little home access to the Internet while those on the highest incomes have high levels of home access. The proportion of households with access also varies considerable with geography and in general terms it is highest in affluent areas and lowest in poorer areas. In essence the emerging picture is one of a divided society in relation to access to the Internet.

The National Statistics (2002) survey reports that people used the Internet for a variety of purposes but in order of popularity in February 2002 people:

- Found general information (74 per cent).
- Sent e-mails (73 per cent).
- Browsed (56 per cent).
- Shopped (42 per cent).
- Found educational information (36 per cent).
- Dealt with financial matters (28 per cent).

- Downloaded software (22 per cent).
- Sought employment (21 per cent).
- Accessed government sites (19 per cent).

The National Statistics survey concentrates on personal use of the Internet; use for work purposes is excluded.

The survey presents a positive image of personal Internet use. However, 44 per cent of adults have never used the Internet. A large majority of this group (72 per cent) indicated that they are very unlikely to access the Internet. This is a very large proportion of the adult population as it represents a third of all adults. The reasons given for this lack of use include:

- Lack of interest (43 per cent).
- No computer or access (25 per cent).
- Lack of confidence and skills (21 per cent).
- No need (17 per cent).

This lack of interest is not new in that the surveys carried out by IT for All (Department of Trade and Industry, 1996; 1997) showed a similar pattern of response which was labelled as alienation. There is clearly a large group of adults who do not see the relevance of ICT to their lives. Declaring that ICT is a new basic skill will not in itself encourage this group to come forward to learn about ICT.

Key points

1. By February 2002, 58 per cent of men and 54 per cent of women had used the Internet.
2. The pattern of access to the Internet is complex and shows that many group are not willing or able to participate. Access is influenced by income (i.e. more likely with higher incomes), geography (i.e. significant regional and national differences across the UK) and age (i.e. 80 per cent of 16 to 24-year-olds use the Internet compared with 12 per cent of adults aged 65 and over).
3. People use the Internet for a variety of purposes but sending e-mail and finding information are major uses.
4. A large majority of non-users (i.e. 72 per cent) have no interest in using the Internet and appear to be unable to see the relevance of ICT to their lives.

Relationship – ICT with literacy and numeracy

There is considerable interest in the use of ICT to support the learning of basic skills. Many organisations have employed ICT programmes as the means of motivating adults to attend basic skills programmes. People appear to be willing to admit to poor ICT skills while they are reluctant to admit to poor literacy and numeracy skills. There is no stigma at the moment from having a lack of computer skills. However, will that remain in a society in which technology is becoming ubiquitous? This is likely to be the situation within a few years, especially when a generation who has had access to ICT throughout their education becomes a significant proportion of the population. It is likely that people with poor technical skills will become stigmatised in a similar way that people with poor basic skills have been.

ICT has been used as a motivational tool. The *Skills for Life* strategy (National Strategy, 2001) reported that half of the adults with poor basic skills would be motivated to improve their skills if it was through computers. However, ICT has more to offer than motivation. It has been used with children and adults to help them to develop their skills including to:

Aid writing
- Assist the development of writing through word processing, by removing the barrier of poor handwriting so that learners can produce a quality document for possibly the first time in their lives.
- Improve spelling and vocabulary through the use of spell checkers and thesauruses.
- Allow writing to be redrafted and corrected.
- The World Wide Web provides many different sources which can provide a resource for writing subjects and topics.

Aid reading
- The World Wide Web provides access to large volumes of reading materials in a wide range of subjects to meet the different interests of the learners.

Aid mathematics

■ Spreadsheets have been employed in many ways to help learners to practice their mathematical skills.

Aid preparation

■ ICT can provide productivity tools for the basic skills tutor to maximise their efforts to prepare for sessions.

Aid assessment

■ ICT can provide the means to assess and record learners' progress.

ICT has been used in many different ways by tutors to aid development of literacy and numeracy skills. Many tutors are integrating learning both ICT and literacy and numeracy together. However, at the moment the skills of tutors to deliver both are probably limited. In some cases ICT has extended the literacy needs of people (e.g. e-mail, text messaging, desktop publishing, keyboard skills, etc.). However, whether this integration is sufficient to label ICT a new basic skill is not clear but there is certainly a contribution towards the change.

A learning group

During a workshop (Taylor, 2002) tutors were asked to consider how ICT could help develop basic skills more effectively, creatively and imaginatively. The list below shows the possibilities:

- Word processing – spell check.
- Art packages – some words, pictures, borders, etc.
- Word processing draft handwriting.
- Dedicated software and websites, for example word games – ESOL packages, opposites, etc. – maths.
- Text messaging (e.g. relevant practical task).
- Hyperstudio – creating multimedia resources (e.g. exciting, highly motivating experience).
- E-mail (e.g. provides the means to communicate with family, friends and colleagues).
- Spreadsheets for budgeting.
- Family learning environment (e.g. children and parents can use ICT together).
- Enjoyable environment, therefore effective.
- Open and flexible learning (e.g. allows learning at a place, pace and time that are more acceptable to the learner).
- ICT makes learning in the community more acceptable.
- Other – videos, cameras and music (e.g. using a camera to record an assignment both motivates and extends its possibilities).
- Links between colleges (e.g. different groups of learners are able to communicate with each other).
- Students' own websites (e.g. creating a website can be a highly motivating and confidence-building experience).

The list includes a very wide range of possibilities of using ICT to aid the development of literacy and numeracy skills. Many exploit the motivational power of technology. Another group were asked how adults with poor basic skills could be helped to learn ICT. The list below shows their additional ideas:

- Additional voluntary peer support.
- Adapt materials.
- Easy, quick tasks.
- E-mail support.

The impact of ICT on literacy itself is an important factor. Keyboard skills are now part of many people's lives from the television remote control, mobile phones, ATMs, tills, weighing machines in supermarkets, video recorders, security locks, calculators, microwave ovens, and washing machines to telephone banking. We all make contact with keyboards and pads in order to function in society. For young people the text message has become part of the way they maintain their social lives. Many small organisations are now able, through low-cost printers and desktop publishing, to publish their own newsletters and other publications.

The nature of the computer interface has also added additional features to visual literacy in that users of ICT need to recognise icons, scroll bars, buttons, menus and toolbars. These have also spread to devices such as mobile phones, symbols on packages, video recorders and music systems. To operate these devices requires a recognition of these visual communication items.

E-mail is the most popular and for many people the most useful communication technology. E-mail messages are a different form of writing to the traditional memo or note. They have a continuous aspect in that the reply can contain the previous message(s) so the whole spectrum of a communication is present. People communicate in a variety of styles using e-mail and often users have to cope with a large number of messages arriving each day, so replies are often short and sometime sharp. Writing skills need to adapt to this new form of communication so that e-mail users can produce short, clear and non-offensive messages.

A website is not described as read but as browsed, indicating the difference in approach with more emphasis on quick scanning and identification than normally required in reading printed material. Browsing requires reading by scanning to identify key words combined with navigating the site through hypertext links. This is a new type of reading and if you are designing websites, a new form of writing. Many new jobs require you to use databases of customer records to both locate information and to enter details of enquiries. Again this is a change in how information is read and written.

The word processor has given everyone the means to write their own letters, reports and memos so that there is now a need for them to also understand layout and presentation of text which previously typists and secretaries undertook. Probably they also corrected grammar, spelling and punctuation for their colleagues. Now everyone needs these new literacy skills.

ICT is changing the requirements of what skills and understanding people need to live and work in the information society. The point where a requirement is identified as literacy or ICT is not obvious in many cases and the relationship is complex.

Key points

1. There is little current stigma in admitting to having poor ICT skills, while there is considerable stigma in saying that you have poor literacy and numeracy skills.
2. Many adults are willing to improve their literacy or numeracy skills if it can be done through, or involving, ICT.
3. ICT can contribute to the development of literacy and numeracy skills through a wide variety of means.
4. ICT has contributed to changing the nature of literacy skills (e.g. keyboard literacy and specialist terms).

How do people currently use ICT?

The National Statistics Omnibus Survey (National Statistics, 2002) considered what people do with access to the Internet for personal motives and showed the trends and importance of certain activities:

	January 2001	February 2002
Using e-mail	65 %	73 %
Finding information	67 %	74 %
Purchasing	30 %	42 %
Financial matters	23 %	28 %
Government	18 %	19 %
General browsing	54 %	56 %

People could indicate more than one item.

In comparison, the US Census Bureau (2001) reported on a survey of how the Internet was used in the home by adults:

Using e-mail	87.7 %
Finding information	64.2 %
Checking news, weather, etc	52.5 %
Job search	19.8 %
Shop or pay bills	39.8 %

Both surveys highlight the importance of e-mail and searching for information. Clearly for individual use the skills and knowledge required to send and receive e-mails and locate information on the World Wide Web are crucial. The other uses of the Internet also demonstrate the integration of online technology into people's lives (e.g. job searching, shopping, financial matters and government). This is probably linked to the rapid growth in websites from almost every type of organisation (e.g. charities, entertainment and public information). Whether the demand for the information or the organisations' desire to present themselves on the World Wide Web came first is difficult to identify.

In terms of ICT skills and understanding, the use of e-mail and finding information requires more than the functional skills of using the applications (e.g. browsers and mail systems). It needs skills such as:

- Searching skills.
- Judging the quality of online information.
- Identifying key words or phrases – is this an ICT or basic skill?
- 'Netiquette' (i.e. online social skills).
- Writing short focused messages – is this an ICT or basic skill?
- Competence with other applications (e.g. word processing, graphics and spreadsheets) so that you can use attachments.

Using e-mail and searching the World Wide Web necessitates more than straightforward functional use of software. It requires a wider range of generic and structural skills (e.g. how you open or save an attachment).

In 2000, Rutland County Council undertook a survey (Rutland Business Survey, 2000) of the IT skills and usage amongst businesses operating in their county. Five hundred and forty-six businesses were interviewed. A large proportion of the businesses could be categorised as small enterprises in that 94 per cent employed less than 25 people. The survey showed that the use of online technologies was very new as a majority of users had started to employ e-mail, obtain Internet accounts or build websites during the last two years. A large proportion of the current non-users intended to begin to use online technologies. Only the businesses employing under ten people showed a reluctance to use technology. A majority of the enterprises using e-mail believed that it had helped their business and a minority now relied on it (i.e. 9 per cent).

The survey identified the ICT skills that enterprises needed. The main ones are:

- E-mail and the Internet (37 per cent).
- Financial management and accounts (21 per cent).
- Databases (21 per cent).
- Spreadsheets (20 per cent).
- Website design (19 per cent).
- Word processing (19 per cent).
- Desktop publishing (14 per cent).
- Keyboard skills (14 per cent).
- Stock control software (14 per cent).
- Presentation software (12 per cent).
- Graphic design/illustrations (9 per cent).
- Project management software (8 per cent).

Communication technology is again the most used ICT function. This is probably not surprising given the growth in e-business and the importance of communication in all forms to an organisation. It does suggest that in any definition of ICT as a skill for life communication technologies must play a key part.

The Rutland list demonstrates the widespread use of ICT in business. Organisations rapidly become dependent on ICT so that when the network crashes many companies are unable to function with any degree of efficiency. It is now acceptable to be told that an organisation cannot answer your query because the network is down.

The list shows the scale of skills and knowledge that businesses now require of employees. It is probably unreasonable to expect this degree of competency of all employees at all times. People will specialise in some areas but it also suggests that individuals will need to be able and willing to learn new skills. In order to maintain a skill requires practice but keeping up to date with even a minority of applications in the Rutland list is probably impossible. The image that emerges is that of an individual who is continually learning new skills, is competent in some applications, is in need of updating with others and has never used other applications. This mix suggests that lifelong learning is a key component of ICT. What makes this image possible is that learners have a solid foundation in ICT with a clear structural understanding combined with the ability to transfer their learning to new situations.

Key points

1. Communication technologies are the most widely used at home and work.
2. E-mail and the Internet are increasingly becoming part of peoples' lives.
3. Communication technologies are new developments to many businesses.
4. Many businesses have benefited from the use of ICT and in some cases have come to rely on it.
5. Businesses require a wide range of ICT skills, covering many different applications.
6. Individuals will need to continuously develop and update their ICT skills and knowledge.
7. People will need a good structural understanding combined with the ability to transfer their learning.

Employment

ICT has already had a major impact on the world of work. Technology is apparent in almost all occupations. Tills are automated and products bar coded. Vegetables are weighed on electronic scales while drivers employ global positioning devices to make their journeys more efficient. Doctors keep their records on computers while almost everyone in an office must now be able to communicate by telephone, fax and e-mail. Expectations of basic ICT skills are now almost a prerequisite to most jobs (Department of Trade and Industry, 2000a). If you scan the vacancy pages of almost any newspaper a large number of the job descriptions will ask for specific ICT skills. Even trainee positions aimed at school or college leavers will frequently require ICT skills and knowledge. A key reason for adults to participate in ICT courses is to find or keep employment (Clarke, 1998; 1999).

John Healey, the then Minister for Adult Skills, stated that more than three quarters of the workforce now used computers as part of their work while 90 per cent of all jobs by 2010 will need IT skills (Healey, 2002). This is even more apparent in terms of new jobs of which 90 per cent will require basic ICT and keyboard skills by 2006 (Jowell, 2001). These statistics demonstrate the fundamental nature of ICT skills for people in employment. ICT skills and understanding are essential for employment. However, ICT includes a wide range of functional, structural and generic skills in the context of a wide range of hardware and software. Job advertisements often specify experience with particular applications rather than more comprehensive definitions.

The UK, with other Western governments, has identified that the future prosperity of their countries relies on a well-educated, flexible workforce that can adapt to change as part of the information or knowledge society. A fundamental part of this new economy is the use of ICT to improve productivity, flexibility and communication. This needs to be at the heart of the knowledge business and so requires a workforce who are competent users of ICT.

The Kent Learning and Business Link theme paper on ICT (The Learning and Business Link Company, 2001) reported that 41 per cent of establishments reporting an ICT skill shortage considered the lack of people with basic ICT skills to be a problem. The paper suggests that people with poor ICT skills are also likely to have poor basic skills. This suggests that combining ICT and basic skills learning programmes would be a useful approach. The *Employer Skill Survey* undertaken by the Department for Education and Skills (2001) reported that employers anticipate the need for more people with ICT related skills over the next two or three years. Thirty-three per cent of establishments will need advanced ICT skills and 21 per cent basic ICT skills. This is not a new factor in that the *Skills Needs in Britain* survey (Department for Education and Skills, 1998) identified computer literacy/IT skills as amongst the main skill gaps. This survey also reported that employees with basic IT skills were likely to be paid more than colleagues without these skills. This shows a similar pattern to comparisons between staff who are literate and numerate with those with poor basic skills.

ICT has now penetrated into a vast range of jobs so that:

- Cleaning supervisors order materials on the Internet and report the hours worked by their team of cleaners by e-mail.
- Foundry foremen produce their production report using word processing.
- Factory workers record their starting and finishing times using smart cards and a keyboard.
- Taxi drivers use technology to communicate with their central control.
- Lorry drivers use computer systems to record their work.
- Receptionists reserve tables in restaurants and book rooms for guests using networked computers.
- Car mechanics search databases for spare parts.

Crowston and Sawyer (2000) considered the influence ICT had on organisations and identified the following areas of impact:

- Changes in industrial structures.
- Organisational outcomes.
- Organisational structures.
- Individuals's work.
- Individual use of ICT.

The overall conclusion is that ICT is now an essential component in many jobs and organisations and its influence continues to have an impact.

Economy

The impact that ICT has on the economy of Great Britain and the world is immense. The OECD (2002) reported that ICT

...contributed significantly to output and productivity growth.

Ford EDAP Internet Café

The report indicated that the market for ICT continues to grow as part of a global market. They estimated that OECD expenditure on ICT was $2.1 trillion in 2001. This illustrates the scale of ICT involvement with the economy of the world.

Communication technology has changed the nature of time and space. E-mail allows you to communicate with people anywhere in the world. It is now possible to employ online tutors who live in a different continent from the learners, but through e-mail communication can function effectively. The ICT skills of an organisation now form part of the competitive advantage that they bring to the market. The level of ICT skill impacts on the individual (gaining and holding onto a job), the company (efficiency and effectiveness of the business) and the competitiveness of the UK as a whole.

E-commerce is rapidly developing and the European Commission:

> *...expects e-commerce in Europe to grow from $17 billion at the end of 1999 to about $360 billion by 2003.*

This demonstrates again the scale and importance of ICT to the European economies. A simple comparison of the costs of sending information between two points illustrates the importance of technology.

The cost of sending a parcel containing 20 lbs of papers from Minnesota to Leicester:

■ Parcel post – $84, 14 days.
■ E-mail – $3, 2 minutes.

In this case access to the Internet had to be paid for at a public access point. The extra advantage that existing e-mails could be read and replied to and that the attachment could also be sent to many other locations at no extra charge further reinforces the power of technology. For individuals, companies, and even countries, the savings through using Internet technology are immense.

However, it needs to be recognised that it is the already wealthy nations who can afford equipment and access who are forging ahead globally:

The UNDP Human Development Report for 1999 notes that a computer would cost the average Bangladeshi the equivalent of eight years wages, while the average American can buy a similar machine for a months salary. (The Centre for Democracy and Technology, 2001, p.6)

It also has to be remembered that some countries are without consistent reliable electricity supplies or access to a telephone line. In some countries the cost of access is still on a per-minute connection basis which can be prohibitively expensive. The success of the Internet in North America is considered to be largely due to the fact that they do not have to pay for individual local calls:

In most developing and transitional economies around the world, fees charged by cybercafés are pegged at 'hard currency' rates, apparently reflecting the assumption that most of the users are overseas visitors; few cybercafés seem to cater to the median citizenry. For instance, A Kiev cybercafé listed on www.cybercafe.kiev.ua charges $6.50/hour, an amount that bars a large part of the local population. (The Centre for Democracy and Technology, 2001, p.9)

In comparison, in the UK there are numerous points of access to ICT where there is either a minimal charge or no charge made, e.g. UK Online Centres, public libraries, etc.

The UN Secretary General Kofi Anan identified the risks of excluding the poorer nations and peoples from ICT (BBC, 1999):

Today, being cut off from basic telecommunication services is a hardship almost as acute as these other deprivations.

ICT professionals

There is a major shortage of ICT professionals in Europe. This is a result of the speed of expansion of ICT in organisations across the European Union. The shortage is not a new phenomenon and National Training Organisations believe that it is still growing although the supply of trained staff has increased (Hillage *et al.*, 2002). The key issue now is not so much the quantity of ICT professionals but rather the quality of skills they can provide. There are approximately one million ICT professionals in Great Britain and their numbers have grown far more rapidly than the rest of the workforce (Institute for Employment Studies, 2001).

The characteristics of the ICT profession (Institute for Employment Studies, 2001) are that:

- there are clusters of ICT professionals in some geographical (e.g. south-east England) and business (e.g. finance) areas;
- women are under-represented in the ICT profession;
- the age of professionals is lower than the rest of the workforce and newer technologies appear to have the youngest workers;
- ICT staff are better qualified than the rest of the workforce; and
- there are more self-employed ICT professionals than in other groups.

Working patterns

Home working has often been associated with low pay and repetitive low skill tasks. ICT has changed the nature of working at home since it allows professional and managerial staff to base their work in their own homes or to operate almost anywhere. It is now a familiar sight to see people using laptop computers on trains, in airports and in almost any location. For many people ICT has blurred the distinction between home and work. It provides organisations and individuals with far more flexibility than was previously possible. This is not always beneficial for the individual, who may find it difficult to stop working. However, the potential to combine work and family responsibilities is substantial.

There has been considerable effort to investigate and develop applications which allow groups to work together. These approaches are often called 'computer-supported cooperative working' (CSCW) and assist groups who will never meet to collaborate across long distances. This allows organisations to reduce the barrier of distance. Design teams can work together without the burden of having to travel long distances to meet. Managers can coordinate their efforts together without the daily or weekly management meeting. Authors can be supported by their editors and publishers while not having to break their concentration to visit them. The immediate gain of computer-supported cooperative working is to make considerable savings in travel costs and time.

Many advantages have been claimed for working at home through ICT, which is often called 'teleworking'. The advantages include:

- Flexible working hours.
- Eliminating travel to work – reduce costs, stress, congestion and save time.
- Reducing the impact of commuting on the environment.
- Family friendly.
- Reducing the need to provide office or other work space.
- Combining different skills and experience more easily.
- Making combining family and work responsibilities.
- Overcoming disabilities or similar barriers.

However, to take advantage of teleworking requires a significant change in working methods and not least being a competent user of ICT. There is also the negative feature of teleworking, such as longer working hours and a blurred distinction between home and work. The Department of Trade and Industry (2000b) suggest that a key skill is "good communication skills – including new skills of communicating across electronic networks". This indicates that the skills are not simply about hardware and software but include more generic skills. In a sense literacy skills have been extended to understanding the nature of writing e-mails, using mailgroups, shared resources and bulletin boards.

There have been many predictions that teleworking would grow very rapidly but often the predictions have been of too large or too quick a change. However, it has grown significantly and the office of National Statistics (2000) reports that there are:

- 312,000 home based teleworkers;
- 805,000 flexible location teleworkers; and
- 477,000 occasional teleworkers (at least one day a week).

This suggests that 5.8 per cent of the employed and self-employed workforce are teleworkers. This is probably an underestimation since it does not include the many people who occasionally work at home or elsewhere using ICT. The figures do indicate that a lack of ICT skills reduces employment opportunities and so has a significant impact on people's lives. This is likely to grow as teleworking spreads and develops. This is not in isolation a sufficient reason for ICT to be considered a basic skill, but it does indicate the impact of a lack of ICT skills in the reduced opportunities available to those people without them.

The Department of Trade and Industry (2000b) identified the ICT skills required for teleworking as:

> *...generic skills, including competence in IT and the use of new communication methods, (for example keyboard skills, use of modems, electronic mail, online discussion, effective use of websites, and the use of software required for the work), report-writing skills and effective telephone communication skills.*

This demonstrates the wide range of ICT-related skills required to be competent. It is not limited to equipment and applications. A key issue is that technical support is often provided by telephone and requires the teleworker or remote worker to undertake tasks which would normally be carried out by technical staff (e.g. carry out tests). Although staff are guided through these tasks they do at least require considerable confidence (e.g. to take off the back of a computer, change connections, etc.).

Teleworking is a two-way process so that it has an impact on people who continue to work in a traditional office or factory setting. They need to be able to effectively communication and collaborate with home- or flexibly-working colleagues. This will require a similar mix of ICT skills as the teleworker and changes the working patterns of the conventional workplace. Without ICT skills in a teleworking/flexible working age people will reduce their employability even if they do not intend to work from home.

Nature of work

The nature of many jobs has been changed and in some cases eliminated by technology (e.g. typing pool). The boundaries between roles have been altered and are still changing. For many people these developments have been largely invisible in that it has been a gradual process and only people returning to employment after a gap have noticed the scale of the transformation. However, many organisations are unable to effectively function without their computer systems. It is now normal to be told that a task cannot be undertaken because the computers are not working.

Structure of organisations

The availability of online information has made organisations flatter, with much of the traditional hierarchy removed. Communication technology allows many variations of organisational structure to be employed. People can work almost anywhere using portable equipment so that concepts such as 'hot-desking' have become the norm in many organisations. The mobile telephone, laptop computer and personal digital assistant (PDA) allow people to work almost anywhere.

Small- and medium-sized enterprises (SMEs)

The growth in the use of the Internet amongst large organisations has been very quick, but slower amongst smaller organisations. However, 55 per cent of all SMEs are now connected to the Internet (Oftel, 2001). Amongst medium-sized organisations (i.e. 51–250 employees), 92 per cent are connected to the Internet, as are 54 per cent of small ones (i.e. 1–50 employees). A further 13 per cent of small organisations are likely to be connected during 2002/2003. These global figures do tend to disguise the difference between the micro-businesses (one employee) and the others. 80 per cent of small businesses employing more than 26 staff are connected, compared to less than 40 per cent with a single employee.

Overall, the picture shows that Internet connectivity is now a part of the majority of SMEs and a large majority of those employing significant numbers of staff. Employees are going to require ICT skills across the entire spectrum of sizes of enterprise. The survey did indicate that 33 per cent of small organisations were either unlikely or did not know if they would connect to the Internet. The reasons given were often that the Internet was not relevant to them. This compares to the response many individuals give to why they are not interested in learning to use ICT. There is possibly some correlation between the two results since the micro-organisations are more likely not to be connected and these probably represent self-employment (i.e. individuals).

Although ICT competence is critical to employability, to be an effective business user of technology also requires some other skills. These include:

- searching for information;
- assessing the quality of online information;
- managing online resources;
- virtual collaborative working;
- presenting/designing information (e.g. presentational graphics); and
- electronic writing (e.g. e-mail).

Key points

1. Three quarters of the workforce now use computers as part of their work while 90 per cent of all jobs by 2010 will need IT skills.

2. Many governments have realised that future prosperity requires a well-educated, flexible workforce that can adapt to change as part of the information or knowledge society. The impact that ICT has on the economy of Great Britain and the world is immense.

3. Employers are expected to need people with technical and user ICT skills over the next few years. ICT is an essential component in many jobs and organisations and its influence continues to grow.

4. There is a major shortage of ICT professionals in Europe. The key issue now is not so much the quantity of ICT professionals but rather the quality of skills they can provide.

5. There are approximately one million ICT professionals in Great Britain and their numbers have grown far more rapidly than the rest of the workforce (Institute for Employment Studies, 2001).

6. ICT is altering the nature of work and in particular the location (e.g. teleworking, 'hot-desking' and mobile working).

7. The use of online information is changing the structure of organisations. In some cases traditional hierarchies are no longer necessary.

8. Access to the Internet is now available to the majority of SMEs and a large majority of larger enterprises.

9. About a third of small organisations are not convinced that the Internet is relevant to them. This compares to a similar proportion of individuals.

e-UK

ICT has already impacted on the government of the UK in similar ways to many other organisations in the changes in working practices. However, communication technologies have caught the imagination of several governments to deliver services, solve problems (e.g. educational attainment) and reduce costs. Successive governments have undertaken many large- and small-scale initiatives to attempt to realise the potential of ICT. Publicity has tended to focus on the problems surrounding some large-scale projects while the successes have attracted little national publicity.

ICT has already extended itself into many areas of peoples lives. There are now digital speed cameras on many roads, databases hold our personal details, postcodes identify us, forms are read by computers, we communicate through mobile phones, interact with our televisions, and many other almost invisible technological influences surround us. This has happened almost without pause over the last two decades and is continuing to grow. The continuous nature of the change has made it almost invisible. Many people come into contact with computer technology daily without being aware of it.

e-Government

The Government is seeking to make access to itself and its processes more open. Taxes can be paid electronically and soon passports, driving licences and benefits will be able to be requested, updated and issued through electronic means. You can e-mail civil servants in many departments and correspond with your Member of Parliament electronically.

The Government has set a series of objectives for the use of ICT to ensure that Great Britain and its people gain the maximum benefits from the digital world. The three main objectives were (e-Envoy, 2002):

- to make the UK the best environment in the world for e-commerce by 2002;
- to ensure that everyone who wants it has access to the Internet by 2005; and
- to make all government services available electronically by 2005.

The Government has made large-scale efforts to achieve these goals. The most visible effort has probably been in relation to public access to the Internet. The UK Online Centres programme has provide over 3,000 ICT centres with an emphasis on providing access in the more deprived communities. The People's Network has equipped libraries with a broadband connection to the Internet for public use. In addition the National Grid for Learning has linked schools to the Internet. These developments represent a major improvement in public access. Local authorities have also been working towards changing the way they communicate with and offer services to their communities who include many vulnerable groups (Hellawell and Mulquin, 2000). By 2003 every council in the UK will have its own website. Many other approaches and initiatives have been tried. These include:

- Connecting community locations/centres to broadband networks.
- Local Government Staff Training Network.
- Electronic Village Halls.
- Business services.
- Wireless Outreach Network.
- Tourist information.
- Availability of educational courses.
- Service information online.

Many of these changes have been quietly received and little public debate has occurred. This is surprising in that government has undertaken national consultations (Raynsford, 2002). The Government are aiming to:

- create a climate in which public service providers will develop their own e-Government programme;
- identify what needs to be done at national level; and
- identify common priorities.

Government has made funds available for local e-Government development including £350 million to enable the target of enabling services to be made available electronically by 2005 (Office of the Deputy Prime Minister, 2002).

Essentially these developments are likely to change the way people interact with government in a significant way. Online access has the potential to allow every citizen to access services without having to visit a government office. This is very beneficial to people living in rural areas, disabled people, carers and the many other groups who have limited mobility. However, it does assume access to and competency with the technology. Without access and competency they will be unable to take advantage of these developments and are essentially disadvantaged. At the moment there is a considerable difference in access to broadband connectivity between urban and rural Britain. Only a small minority of the rural population can access broadband while a large majority of urban inhabitants can.

The history of technological change has often been accompanied by change in face-to-face facilities. At the moment the e-Government developments are additional to existing services. However, past experience of technological change has shown that the temptation to rationalise services especially when savings can be made are enormous. How long will e-Government remain additional? If services are only available online then people who are unable to use ICT systems will be seriously disadvantaged.

e-Democracy

The Hansard Society (2002) give a variety of reasons for their e-democracy programme which serve as a set of reasons for considering why the use of ICT could aid democracy. They include:

- To decrease the feeling of remoteness between politicians and their electorate.
- To connect politicians and citizens and thus increase representation.
- To allow people to contribute to parliamentary business.

The potential for ICT to enhance democracy has been extensively discussed. In simple terms communication technologies make it easier to communicate with our representatives at local or national level. However, this potential brings into sharp focus the unequal access and use of ICT. This disadvantage means a large part of the population cannot take advantage of this new method of communication. In contrast ICT can allow groups to provide information to our representatives who normally would be unable to communicate (e.g. women victims of domestic violence, see Coleman and Normann, 2000). This equation that ICT is both a force for social exclusion and inclusion has been identified by many writers and researchers (Clarke, 2002b). It poses a dilemma in many contexts. Should a Member of Parliament give precedent to answering e-mail or traditional post from their constituents?

Already Internet users have advantages over other citizens. A visit to the House of Commons' website gives you access to a list of all Members of Parliament, a link to their e-mail if they have an address (as an overwhelming majority do) and, in many cases, access to their personal websites. In addition you can obtain copies of research reports to download from the Commons library, links to the Ombudsman, access to copies of Acts of Parliament, Government Press Releases and many other services or sources of information. This single example demonstrates that ICT users have an advantage over other citizens who could probably acquire the same information conventionally but would need to spend far more time and probably funds to achieve the same result. It is often the case that the electronic publication is free or available at a lower cost than the printed version.

Parity (2002) undertook a survey of the use of e-mail by Members of Parliament. This showed that the majority of members prefer to deal with correspondence through traditional means rather than by using e-mail. However, a large volume of correspondence is undertaken through the use of e-mail. Parity reported that 90 per cent of MPs carried out up to a quarter of their correspondence through e-mail. A quarter of all MPs receive more than 25 e-mails per week and 6 per cent receive more than 50 e-mails. The experience from organisations who have introduced e-mail is that its use grows continually and has a considerable impact on more traditional forms of communication. If this experience is repeated with MPs then citizens who do not use or have access to e-mail may find themselves at a disadvantage.

These are relatively immediate uses of ICT to enhance democracy but other more radical functions have been experimented with and are likely to grow. The political debate has been placed online in terms of the main political parties having websites, an occasional webcast has been tried and descriptions of candidates do appear on their own websites. This is a fairly modest use and it will probably grow unevenly both between candidates and parties (i.e. some will be more enthusiastic than others). Experiences from the USA suggest that fringe and independent candidates have benefited from being early adopters of campaigning online.

The potential for candidates to hold online meetings with the voters is real and will allow far more communication than conventional meetings or one-way broadcasts. Online meetings allow everyone equal opportunity to ask questions and to take part in the debate. Large numbers of voters could genuinely have contact with candidates so could make informed decisions. This type of development on a sufficiently large scale might revitalise interest in political life that has fallen if measured in terms of votes cast. However, without access to ICT and the skills to use them people will be unable to take part and so will be disadvantaged. Citizenship is a fundamental right of all adults so any change that reduces access to knowledge impacts on this right.

The cost of creating a website or providing online communication is relatively low compared to paying for newspaper, poster or television broadcasts so that a change in the balance of political communication to favour the Web may well encourage smaller parties to be more active. In the USA independent candidates have used the Internet to effectively reach voters. Without ICT skills people will again be unable to contribute as effectively to a party of their choice or to become a candidate.

Voting online has already been tried on a local small scale for referendum-type activities and in local elections. It is hoped that by making it possible to vote over the Internet, more people will want to vote and the low turnouts at local, General and European Elections will be reversed. In the 2001 General Election only 59.4 % of the registered voters voted. This is the lowest turnout since universal adult suffrage was introduced. However, again the catch is access and ICT competency. Without access or competency a person cannot take advantage of online voting.

The Office of the Deputy Prime Minister (2002) discusses the possibilities of an e-enabled general election within the foreseeable future (i.e. 2008 or 2011) employing a range of technology (e.g. mobile phones, digital television and Internet). These changes are intended to add extra ways of voting rather than alter the tradition polling station visit. They are fundamental to democracy and are certainly significant in terms of the possible impact on people's basic rights.

The evidence (Office of the Deputy Prime Minister, 2002) relating to e-voting is partial in that there have been very few experiments. The limited evidence suggests that there is support for e-voting to be made available. Perhaps not surprisingly this is more apparent amongst existing Internet users. The possible impact on voting is significant with many (21 per cent) non-voters claiming that polling arrangements are inconvenient and that they would have voted if they could do so over the telephone (Electoral Commission, 2001).

Key points

1. Government has already been changed by ICT in similar ways to many other organisations (e.g. working practices).
2. The Government is seeking to make access to itself and its processes more open through ICT.
3. The Government has set a series of objectives for the use of ICT to ensure that Great Britain and its people gain the maximum benefits from the digital world.
4. The possibilities that ICT brings to democracy have been extensively debated (e.g. electronic voting, e-mailing MPs and Local Counsellors or access public information) and are emerging.
5. E-mail is emerging as a significant means of communication between citizens and their representatives.
6. The use of online communication to support campaigning is still minor.

e-Learning

There is considerable interest and development underway across all education sectors in Great Britain to exploit the potential for ICT to support and deliver learning. Currently they represent a relatively small proportion of the total learning opportunities provided for adults. However, the pace of development is rapid and e-learning is identified as the means of expanding provision by overcoming the barriers of place, pace and time. That is, you can study where you want to, at the speed that is appropriate to you and at a convenient time for you. In July 2003, the document *Towards a Unified e-Learning Strategy* was published to consult the whole of the education sector on a long-term government strategy for e-learning. (Department of Education and Skills, 2003b).

The Learning and Skills Council's Distributed and Electronic Learning Group (2002) investigated the potential of e-learning to deliver and support learning. The group identified e-learning as a vital component in learning and skills. They recognised its potential to reach new learners and to deliver learning in areas such as literacy and numeracy skills. The *Success For All* (Department for Education and Skills, 2002) consultation document on the future of Further Education and Training identified that ICT was a powerful way of motivating learners and delivering learning. However, the DELG report (DELG, 2002) identified a lack of research evidence to support the development of e-learning. This is widely recognised as a risk factor in realising the potential of e-learning. However, some studies have indicated that successful e-learners are confident, motivated people with a previous record of educational achievement. If you lack ICT skills it is unlikely that you will be a confident and motivated e-learner.

Learndirect is a major government-supported initiative to make vocational e-learning available to the whole population by creating a national network of learning centres. In June 2002 (Learndirect, 2002) there were 1,691 centres open, delivering 621 e-learning courses and 362,000 learners. Learndirect is growing very quickly, expanding courses, centres and learners. A key objective of Learndirect is to widen participation in learning and it targets many disadvantaged groups and individuals. These groups are often associated with limited access to and use of ICT. Learndirect provides individual support to learners either in the learning centres or online.

Drop-in ICT learning (WEA, Manchester)

The Open University has been developing its online services and by June 2002 160,000 students and tutors were online using e-mail to communicate. 80,000 assignments are submitted electronically (i.e. about 10 per cent of the total) and 178 courses require students to have online access (Open University, 2002). Open University courses last at least six months and in many cases several years, while Learndirect courses are mainly short, their duration being measured in hours.

Almost every university has some e-learning development underway and although they currently represent a small proportion of the total learning they undertake, they are growing rapidly. New international online universities have been launched (e.g. Capella University) and are growing swiftly, in some cases at 100 per cent a year.

National Learning Network (NLN) is a national initiative that has initially concentrated on further education colleges, assisting them to employ information and learning technology (ILT) within their courses. This is a wider use of technology in learning than e-learning. ILT has been used to integrate technology into conventional approaches so is about a very wide spread use of technology rather than creating a new form (i.e. e-learning or online learning). It is therefore potentially likely to make the use of ICT more important to learners than e-learning in the near future. That is, they will come into contact with it more frequently. From April 2003, the NLN is being extended into Adult and Community Learning and Specialist colleges.

There is a long history of the use of computer-based learning in large organisations. Many large financial companies were amongst the first to adopt computer-based learning and have continued to support and develop the methods. Several major organisations have launched corporate universities based on the use of communication technologies. Learndirect targets small- and medium-sized enterprises and has many courses specifically for business. Several e-learning approaches have been developed for business including Just in Time Training, which is based on the concept of workers accessing training when they need it at their workplace. However, this again assumes that the learners are competent and confident users of ICT. The large companies are supported by many specialist enterprises who develop generic and bespoke learning products for them.

ICT was introduced into schools during the 1980s and significant investments have since been made in integrating ICT into education. The National Grid for Learning has provided access to the Internet for all schools while teachers have been trained in the use of ICT in education. These developments are intended to ensure the advantages of ICT in learning are made available to all children. Many adults take part in ICT courses in order to be able to assist their children and enabled them to take advantage of ICT in their education (Clarke, 1999).

Children who do not have access to or support with ICT at home are likely to be at a disadvantage compared to other children, in a similar way that children of households without books are disadvantaged. ICT competence is therefore a family concern to assure that children are not disadvantaged in their school work.

Using multimedia CD-ROMs in a learning centre (Hillcroft College)

Although ICT skills and knowledge are important for taking part in e-learning or ILT, learners also need a range of more generic skills to be effective. These include (Clarke, 2002a):

- acceptance of responsibility;
- self-management;
- communication;
- self-assessment;
- collaborative working;
- electronic writing;
- electronic reading and note-taking;
- research and searching skills; and
- analysis.

The ICT skills required by students were identified by Pettigrew and Elliott (1999) and include:

- word processing;
- spreadsheets;
- graphs and charts;
- drawing and manipulating graphics;
- presentation graphics;
- e-mail;
- browsing the World Wide Web;
- file management; and
- navigating computer systems to locate and use information.

This combination of generic and ICT skills essentially form the e-learning skills required to be a successful learner. The e-Learning Task Force (2002) report recommended that by 2010 everyone should have access to ICT as a basic skill in part, to enable them to have the opportunities provided by e-learning.

Key points

1. There is enormous interest in employing ICT to support and deliver learning. Many universities, colleges, Learndirect, training providers and adult education providers are making significant progress in using e-learning.
2. E-learning represents only a small proportion of the total learning opportunities provided for adults, but is growing rapidly.
3. E-learning has been identified as having the potential to motivate learners, remove some of the barriers socially disadvantaged adults face and deliver learning.
4. Although ICT skills and knowledge are important for taking part in e-learning or ILT, learners also need a range of more generic skills to be effective (e.g. learning skills).

Everyday life

ICT has and is changing the way we live our lives. We have access to vast information resources and can communicate almost instantly with our friends, family and work colleagues. People expect that everyone has a mobile phone and, in many cases, access to computers and the Internet. We can obtain funds from cash machines at any time of day or night, pay bills whenever we want to and work from home as easily as from our formal work place. It is the age of the instant result, so that tolerance of delay is very much reduced.

ICT is now part of everyone's lives. It has become so much a part of life that it has become almost invisible. Few people would consciously notice that railway information is provided through an electronic display, that tourist information is available through a touch display and that public libraries control the issue of books through a computer. It is now part of the world in which we operate.

Attitudes

The Motorola report (MORI, 2000) is a survey carried out by MORI to investigate the attitudes in Great Britain towards technology. It provided an insight into these attitudes, particularly amongst users of technology. It showed that technology was now part of the British life experience. People were now using technology to provide security for their family (e.g. mobile phone), to conduct financial affairs, to shop online, to access learning and to develop relationships (e.g. online chatting).

A major part of online technology is being able to interact with other people through e-mail, conferencing and chat rooms. Communication is a major advantage of technology. People can socialise online, conduct business, learn new knowledge and communicate in many different ways. Cummings *et al.* (2002) reported on the quality of online communications to carry out social relationships compared to face-to-face and telephone communications. Online communication is a powerful means of developing social relationships but is not as effective as face-to-face or telephone communications. This is perhaps not a surprise given the relatively short period we have had to assimilate online communication methods.

The DfEE's benchmark study (Department for Education and Employment, 2001) reported that 44 per cent of the population regard computers as very important in their lives and 73 per cent of parents believed that computer skills were essential for their children now and 98 per cent believed they would be in the future. However, the study revealed different attitudes to computers depending on age, class and income. In agreement with the National Statistics surveys, attitudes and use were skewed. Younger professional users were likely to spend more time using the Internet than older and poorer people.

The attitudes of non-users are interesting in that the majority are not planning to learn to use ICT in the future. Only a minority are motivated to learn about ICT. This again demonstrates a substantial minority who do not identify with ICT.

The attitudes of teachers towards ICT is especially important in that they are likely to influence their students and are vital to the realisation of the potential of ICT to assist learning. They may also indicate the attitudes of other professional groups. School teachers have received considerable support with developing their ICT skills through the New Opportunities Fund. Further education, university and adult and community tutors have or will receive assistance as well, although on a more modest basis. Williams *et al.* (1998) reported on the attitude of school teachers to ICT. They stated that an overwhelming majority of teachers were interested in improving their ICT skills and knowledge. However, many teachers were concerned about their ability to keep up with ICT developments, in particular the development of their own students. Some teachers were worried about the effort required to realise the benefits of e-learning. The survey showed that attitudes were not linked to teaching experience.

Most people would agree that being able to read, write and use numbers are skills that are relevant to their lives. This is not yet the case with ICT. In a sense a large group of people are voting with their feet that ICT is not a basic or fundamental skill to them. However, this is likely to change with widening access to the technology, expansion of services available online, improvements in the design of the technology (i.e. more user friendly) and growth of digital television (i.e. providing access to the Internet). Attitudes do change and ICT is still relatively new compared to other technological developments such as telephones and television, which took far longer to be universally accepted and available.

Health

Online sites offering information on health are amongst the most popular accessed by users: so much so that the European Union is developing a set of quality criteria for health websites (e-health, 2002). The National Health Service has a strategy for providing the public with advice on health issues (NHS, 1998). NHS Direct and Direct

Online offer information on health and lifestyles through a telephone and online service. Several healthy living initiatives employ communication technologies to disseminate their messages. General Practitioners now keep health records on computer and many health centres are using their own websites to provide patients with access to information as well as allowing appointments to be made by e-mail.

Without ICT skills these additional services are barred and patients must rely on the information being duplicated in conventional forms such as leaflets, notice boards, books and from their doctor. This is far less available than an online source which can be updated in a few minutes and does not require a printer or distribution system. New information can be made quickly available online. Health newsgroups provide access to people with similar health problems to offer mutual support. New research is often initially published on the World Wide Web and there is often a significant delay before it appears in print; even then it will appear in specialist journals not generally available to the public. In contrast, websites are freely accessible.

Shopping

In many communities it is now a familiar sight to see supermarket vans delivering the family shopping which has been ordered online. Many people have found that it can save them time to order their groceries over the Internet rather visit the shop in person. The weekly shop is a fundamental part of family life. At the moment there is little or no financial advantage to supermarket shopping online, but in other aspects of online shopping discounts are offered. If people are unable to take advantage of what has become a normal aspect of life through a lack of skill then ICT is a basic skill.

A quarter of the population (MORI, 2001) have bought goods over the Internet. The characteristics of Internet shoppers tend to reflect the people who have access, and so are skewed towards more affluent parts of the population. In the same way the advantages identified reflect people with higher incomes and limited spare time. However, a significant majority (78 per cent) of the population are aware that you can buy goods over the Internet. This high level of awareness remains high both in terms of age and social class across the population.

Banking and buying books are the most likely goods and services to be bought over the Internet (MORI, 2001). However, a wide range of other products and services are purchased including food, compact discs, travel (i.e. air and rail), holidays, cinema tickets, hotels, cars, computer hardware and clothes. Internet shopping is closely linked to access to and use of the Internet; therefore as this expands, shopping is also likely to grow.

The US Department of Commerce reported that online retail shopping increased by 19 per cent from 2000 to 2001. Slyke *et al.* (2002) considered the differences between men and women's perception of web-based shopping. They reported that both men and women are equally likely to use the Internet. However, men are more likely to buy goods than women online.

Adults who are socially or economically disadvantaged are often unable to take advantage of modern shopping methods (e.g. out-of-town shopping and hypermarkets) because of a lack of transport. They are therefore unable to take advantage of lower prices and wider choice that is often associated with retail parks and other modern shopping approaches. Internet shopping is a new development which is likely to widen choice, lower costs and increase convenience as it expands. Without the skills to use the Internet, disadvantaged people will be further deprived thus potentially having a significant impact on their lives. With ICT, a lack of transport can at least be partially removed.

Publishing

In any community there are many people who produce original writings, artwork or other forms of self expression. The traditional problem faced by any creative person is to make their work available to others, that is, to get their work published. ICT provides a means of making publishing possible for almost anyone or any community, either as a desktop-published or online document. However, it does assume that the people have the necessary skills. These include:

- functional skills of using web page applications and tools;
- functional skills for desktop publishing;
- functional skills for computer art;
- understanding the structure of the World Wide Web;
- understanding of hypermedia;
- web page design; and
- writing for online reading.

Many of these skills are far from basic and fall more into the category of advanced skills. This view of publishing is essential based on producing free publications or being your own publisher. There is also the growing e-book publishing industry which offers new authors and those who are specialist writers the opportunity to earn an income from their work. This is based on a new model of the relationship between writer and publisher with the rights of the author substantially increased in comparison to the conventional relationship. Publications are made available as electronic and/or printed documents as part of a POD (Print On Demand) system, which allows individual books to be produced. There are thus opportunities for artists to earn a living from their work if they are ICT literate.

A final consideration of electronic publications is that the trend towards e-books provides a new form of information which is only available to ICT-literate users. E-books are often available at lower costs and many e-publications are only available online.

Information

All users of the World Wide Web rapidly begin to appreciate its value in simply providing access to information. Often people value the information that makes their lives easier rather than sophisticated research reports. So access to information is prized in relation to:

- Train timetables.
- Holiday and tourist information.
- Maps.
- Booking concerts or other events.
- Product data to aid purchasing decisions.
- Health information.
- Government data.
- Broadcasters.

Nowadays almost every television and radio programme has a website where you can learn more, interact with the broadcasters or gain an insight into the programme. The use of the Internet to purchase tickets is rapidly increasing with a rise from 12 per cent in January 2001 to 42 per cent in February 2002 (National Statistics, 2002). Simple access to information is important to people so that non-users or people with no access are seriously disadvantaged.

To benefit from the World Wide Web requires users who are able to

- browse the Web (e.g. navigation within and across different sites);
- search for information;
- assess the quality of information; and
- use the technology competently (i.e. hardware and software).

The Internet is now a major planning tool for people's social lives. When you are planning a trip the Internet provides you with information about the journey, places to visit, maps, hotels and many other types of information. It is now normal to be sent the address of a website rather than a brochure about a location. Many organisations have established websites with the express purpose of communicating with their customers and do not provide an alternative method. It is likely that this will grow since it is a far cheaper way of providing information. People with no ICT skills will be unable to access this information and increasingly will have narrower choices.

Public ICT centre

Recreation

ICT is often associated with games. Normally this takes the form of young people playing computer games. This is certainly a major use of computers especially amongst younger adults. However, there is a far wider spectrum of entertainment available from ICT. These include:

- DVD – many movies are now available on DVD so that you can watch them at home.
- Webcasts – celebrities broadcasting online so that potentially millions of people can interact with them and ask questions as if they were in the same room. Webcasts are also used for educational and business purposes.

- Many television and radio programmes now have associated websites. Some live programmes have created links to dynamic websites so that viewers and listeners can interact with the programme.
- Some radio broadcasts are available online.
- Online gaming allows people to interact through a game in the same way that they could if in the same room while being separated by half the world.
- Museums, art galleries and libraries have now established themselves on the World Wide Web so that people can visit them from their own homes.

The growth of online- and ICT-based entertainment is another trend demonstrating how ICT is becoming part of people's lives.

Ubiquitous computing

Computers are often described as ubiquitous. That is, they are in all parts of the world in which we live. Computer technology now forms part of many everyday objects. If wanting to get some money from a bank we will visit a cash machine, which is essentially a networked computer. A visit to a supermarket, theatre or simply telephoning a supplier will bring us into contact with ICT. Our shopping habits are analysed by a computer application, our details are stored on a database, and are used by direct mail/telephone companies to identify us as potential customers.

At home we are unable to escape computer technology since many familiar appliances incorporate ICT such as:

- cordless telephones;
- microwave ovens;
- music systems; and
- burglar alarms.

People are often unaware of this overwhelming presence of technology but they may well be at a disadvantage if they do not understand ICT. The key to many issues is the ability of the individual to make informed choices. Without ICT skills and knowledge people cannot make informed choices.

Key points

1. ICT has and is changing the way we live our lives. This is probably accelerating.

2. Online communication is a powerful means of developing social relationships but is not as effective as face-to-face or telephone communications.

3. Almost half of the population regard ICT as being very important to their lives while a large majority of parents believe that computer skills were essential for their children.

4. Attitudes to computers depend on age, class and income of the individual.

5. Online sites offering information on health are amongst the most popular accessed by users.

6. A quarter of the population have bought goods over the Internet (MORI, 2001). The US Department of Commerce reported that online retail shopping increased by 19 per cent from 2000 to 2001.

7. ICT offers the opportunity to allow many people who produce original writings, artwork or other form of self-expression to have them published.

8. The Internet now plays a major part in providing information for people's lives (e.g. timetables, traffic news, places to visit, maps, hotels and many other types of information).

9. Online- and ICT-based entertainment is expanding rapidly.

10. It is almost impossible to live in Great Britain and not come into contact with computer technology.

11. People are concerned with keeping up with the ICT pace of change.

Digital divide

Information and Communication Technology (ICT) has the potential to contribute towards overcoming social exclusion by assisting disadvantaged individuals to take an active part in the community. Yet, it can further disadvantage and exclude people if they are not able to take advantage of technological developments.

Many people who are socially disadvantaged do not have access to technology, are unaware of its benefits to them and are not skilled in its use. It is therefore not a simple task for them to benefit from ICT.

Many of the images presented of ICT show individuals working at home on their own computers. However, for many disadvantaged people this is unrealistic as they are likely to be dependent on public ICT centres and facilities. Home ownership and use is skewed by gender, income, age and educational attainment (National Statistics, 2001; Home Office Partnership, 1999; Clarke, 1998; Measuring Information Society, 1997). Thus, the young professional man is the stereotypical home computer user.

Many reports and investigations have identified the disparity of access to ICT that is often referred to as the 'digital divide'. The Learning and Skills Council's Distributed and Electronic Learning Group (Learning and Skills Council, 2002) recommended that:

> *In view of the disparities in provision across the wide range of providers encompassed within the Council's remit, we recommend that the Council urgently address the need to ensure effective access to e-learning infrastructure and provision among all its provider organisations, within the overall capital investment programme.*

The Social Exclusion Unit (Department of Trade and Industry, 2000) identified that

> *...there are gaps in provision and barriers still exist which prevent people in deprived neighbourhoods accessing ICTs.*

It is clear that public access to ICT is very important to ensure that many people are not excluded. Freedom to use the equipment on demand with the minimum of restrictions is needed. Public access to the Internet and computer facilities is growing rapidly through libraries, UK Online Centres, Learndirect, telecottages, local authorities, colleges and cybercafés. However, it is probably fair to say that many adults would still find it difficult to gain access to a computer within a reasonable distance from their homes. The e-Envoy (2002) provides a comparison between public access points in the UK and other European nations. This shows that although we have thousands of sites in terms of access per thousand inhabitants we are behind countries such as Finland, Germany, Ireland and Belgium.

This large and continuing growth in public access is only useful if adults are confident and competent users of ICT. They have to overcome the major barrier of entering a learning centre or other ICT location. Anecdotal evidence suggests that this is a significant barrier to many adults who are socially or economically disadvantaged. Once inside the centre the person must be able to transfer skills learned elsewhere to the new situation and perhaps different versions, or completely new applications. It is only necessary to observe a learner who is able to browse the Web with Internet Explorer, encounter Netscape Navigator, or even an earlier version of Internet Explorer to realise transfer is not easy or immediate. UK Online Centres and Peoples' Network sites provide support to help users to overcome these barriers.

Earlier we discovered that approximately a third of adults do not see the relevance of ICT to their lives. If we are to avoid a society divided by information technology then we need to find ways of making them aware of the role ICT could play in their lives and the benefits they could gain. There have been several national programmes to encourage learning about ICT such as:

- BBC's *Computers Don't Bite*.
- BBC's *Webwise*.
- BBC's *Becoming Webwise*.
- *IT for All* (Government).
- *UK Online* (Government).

These have all been successful but the scale of the task and the short-term nature of the initiative have largely left the task unfinished. To attract and train the millions of people who need ICT skills will require a prolonged effort over many years. The recent substantial investment in basic skills has been aimed at the reported 7 million adults with literacy or numeracy difficulties. Approximately 24 million adults (Cybrarian Project, 2002) require ICT skills and, in a similar way to basic skills, require to be persuaded to take part. A similar investment is needed to provide the learning opportunities to enable the millions of people to acquire basic ICT skills.

Community ICT course (Swarthmore, Leeds)

Key points

1. ICT has the potential to contribute towards overcoming social exclusion.
2. Socially disadvantaged people often do not have access to technology, are unaware of its benefits to them and are not skilled in its use.
3. Ownership of ICT is skewed by gender, income, age and educational attainment.
4. Public access to ICT is critical for many socially and economically disadvantaged people.
5. This large and continuing growth in public access is only useful if adults are confident and competent users of ICT.
6. National initiatives have proved effective in encouraging people to learn about ICT.

Community

ICT has potentially two major impacts on communities:

1. As a catalyst for neighbourhood and community development.
2. As a new form of community.

ICT can play an important role in neighbourhood renewal (Shearman, 1999). ICT has been used a catalyst to bring people together in order to develop their communities. Many villages, urban communities and groups have established websites which serve as local notice boards, newsletters and as a source of local information. Rural communities are often disadvantaged by their dispersed nature combined with factors such as a lack of coordination between service providers. ICT is particularly important in rural communities to overcome these problems (Neighbourhood Renewal Unit, 2001).

The Government's New Opportunities Fund and various European initiatives have provided substantial resources to encourage ICT development within communities. These have included:

- Wired Communities;
- Digital Communities;
- UK Online Centres;
- Community Grids for Learning;
- Electronic Village Halls; and
- Telecottages.

Online communities are not limited by geography or time. It is possible for people in all parts of the world to communicate. Messages can be sent at any time and equally read whenever it is convenient to the individual. These factors encourage new forms of community to grow such as communities of interest. People who share an interest (e.g. genealogy) or need (e.g. who suffer from the same illness) can communicate, cooperate, and essentially form a community. The Internet started as a means of widening academic communities so this is a natural development. These are largely communities of individuals (Wellman, 2001).

Families with members who live in different parts of the world can maintain their links through e-mail easier than if they live in the same country. Ethnic minorities can maintain their languages and culture by connecting with each other and online newspapers so that geographical barriers are reduced. The communication means take a variety of forms such as mailgroups in which messages are shared across the entire community, bulletin boards where people visit online sites to share information, chat rooms and direct e-mail between people.

Online communities can take on many forms and serve a wide range of purposes. Conventional communities are often described in terms of their geographical area, population (e.g. age, gender, ethnic origin, etc.) and shared objectives. Individuals are often members of many different communities. Online communities are more difficult to describe since boundaries are often vague and ill-defined. A group of people sharing a single hobby can be described as a community even though their interaction is limited to an occasional e-mail message. Others are far more substantial with a wide range of shared aims, active cooperation and many activities (Preece, 2001).

People are socially equal online and can present themselves in any way they want. People can have a voice online that would not be readily available through any other media. People can express their opinions about issues which they would never have the opportunity to do, or to question politicians in a way that would be impossible conventionally. Communication technology transcends many of the barriers people face in their lives but without ICT skills they are excluded from participating.

Community outreach – Primary School, Bradford

Community outreach – Church Hall, Shap

Key points

1. ICT can be a powerful influence on community development by being a catalyst for change.
2. Communication technologies can provide a new form of community (e.g. communities of interest). Online communities are not limited by geography or time.
3. People are socially equal online and can present themselves in any way they want.

Defining ICT skills

Earlier we concluded that a definition of basic ICT would need to include:

- functional knowledge;
- structural understanding; and
- generic skills

in the context of a wide range of hardware and software applications and systems. In this section we will seek to add depth to this outline statement.

Functional knowledge

1. Keyboard skills.
2. Hardware skills (i.e. operating computers, printers, modems, scanners and digital cameras safely. This includes simple maintenance such as changing the paper or cartridges in a printer and connecting equipment to the computer).
3. Applications (i.e. using a range of software applications appropriately such as word processors, spreadsheets, databases, web page editors, desktop publishing, graphics, browsers and search engines).
4. Operating systems (i.e. using an operating system to manage files and folders).
5. Present information effectively.
6. Locate information effectively.

Structural understanding

1. Transferable skills and knowledge.
2. Understanding the difference between operating system and applications' functions.
3. Understanding the structure of the Internet.
4. Identifying hardware and software problems.
5. Understanding the structure of the World Wide Web.
6. Understanding of hypermedia.
7. Understanding the design/structure of websites/pages.

Generic skills

1. Electronic writing (e.g. e-mail).
2. Online discussion including 'netiquette' (i.e. the social skills).
3. Effective use of websites.
4. Assessing the quality of information.
5. Searching the Web.
6. Time management.
7. Problem solving.
8. Searching for information.
9. Assessing the quality of online information.
10. Managing online resources.
11. Virtual collaborative working.
12. Presenting/designing information (e.g. presentational graphics).
13. Acceptance of responsibility.
14. Self-management.
15. Self-assessment.
16. Collaborative working.
17. Reading and note-taking.
18. Research and searching skills.
19. Analysis.
20. Learning skills.
21. Writing for online reading.
22. Designing publications.

This is a list that includes foundation, intermediate and advanced skills. The foundation requirement needs to include the skills and understanding that are required to assist the individual to be able to increase their knowledge, understanding and skills. Adult literacy and numeracy standards are defined against a range of levels, with three entry levels before level 1 which aligns with other standards. The standard for level 1 ICT has been defined as a key skill and in the form of a number of ICT qualifications such as New CLAIT. These do not assume any prior experience of ICT.

Key skill ICT

This is based on the user being able to:

- find;
- explore;
- develop; and
- present

information in the form of text, images and numbers (QCA, 2002). The emphasis is on the user choosing and using their ICT skills. At level 1, basic information is used in the context of short straightforward tasks.

New CLAIT

New CLAIT consists of a mandatory unit "Using the Computer" and optional units (Clarke, 2002c; OCR, 2002a,b). In order to achieve the certificate learners must complete five units (i.e. the one mandatory unit and four other units). The optional units cover a wide range of applications and unit 11 is the BBC's course *Becoming Webwise*. The other units include word processing, spreadsheets, databases, graphs and charts, presentation graphics, electronic communication, web page creation, computer art and desktop publishing. The mandatory unit is focused on using a computer and managing files. The standard also encourages its delivery in the context of understanding issues such as copyright, data protection and the environment.

New CLAIT recognises that there are a wide range of applications available as part of ICT. The wide range of applications essentially shows the range of contexts in which ICT is used. By providing a choice of units the qualification allows learners to customise the qualification to suit their needs and context.

Group of ICT learners

Entry level ICT

The question is whether the existing level 1 definitions of ICT are sufficient or if an entry level standard is also required. A large part of the population do not use ICT, are not interested in it, and do not see the relevance of ICT to their lives. Several studies and many sources of anecdotal evidence suggest that the first step is to build learners' confidence and motivation to learn about ICT in any learning programme. The entry level could therefore be defined in these terms.

An approach that has been found to be effective in motivating adults to take part in learning is the short taster event which aims to show people what they can learn and the relevance of the subject to them. Both are critical for ICT. Since both home and business ICT users widely use e-mail and the Internet, perhaps this would be the right context to offer taster type or other entry level events.

The other key factor is that ICT is continuously changing and developing so it is vital that the concept of transferability of skills is introduced in an appropriate way. Entry level 1 thus becomes concerned with confidence, relevance and transferability.

Is a single entry level sufficient so that a learner would progress from the entry level to level 1? For many people that would be perfectly feasible, but for people returning to learning after a long interval or having limited confidence in themselves then further entry levels might well serve a useful purpose. They could continue to build confidence, relevance and transferable skills through concentrating on issues such as:

- Basic language of ICT.
- Starting up and switching off a computer and other equipment.
- Using a mouse or similar input device.
- Using a keyboard.
- Using an operating system (e.g. help system).
- Using applications.
- Opening and closing applications.

These are important skills but perhaps not the most fascinating, so given the vital nature of continuing the process of confidence and motivational development the context in which these are offered is critical. Current practice is often based on:

- Making the process fun by using games to practice using input devices such as a keyboard and mouse.
- Using multimedia CD-ROMs.
- Searching the Internet.
- Taking photographs or using a scanner to add images to documents.

All these methods allow the learners to familiarise themselves with operating systems and the physical nature of computer equipment in an interesting and motivational way.

Key points

1. Basic ICT skills need to be defined in terms of functional, structural and generic skills.
2. Existing ICT standards partially meet the needs of basic ICT.
3. ICT entry level standards will be needed.

Conclusions

At the beginning of this analysis we identified the main areas of impact that poor literacy, numeracy and language skills had on individuals. Low levels of ICT skills are beginning to have a similar impact on people:

1. *Income.* ICT is becoming a fundamental requirement in almost all employment. A lack of ICT skills is likely to result in finding it more difficult to get a job and to limit opportunities in the workplace. Almost certainly people will face periods of unemployment and low-paid employment without ICT skills. The nature of employment is being changed by the introduction of ICT so that this effect is likely to grow until it may not be possible to work without ICT skills.

2. *Employment.* ICT is changing the nature of employment so that more flexible working is now possible. Many jobs will require people to operate with a laptop computer and mobile phone on a hot-desk basis. Again, without ICT skills people will have reduced opportunities. People without ICT skills will be excluded from the possibilities of teleworking. One of the main reasons for adults taking part in ICT courses is to improve their employment opportunities.

3. *Economy.* The economy of Great Britain is significantly influenced by the ability of companies and organisations to exploit ICT. This is directly related to individuals being competent users of ICT. A population with limited ICT skills is likely to impact on the economy by reducing the ability of the country to compete.

4. *Health.* A lack of ICT skills means that the additional features offered by the NHS, news groups and individual General Practitioner's websites will not be available so that individuals will be poorer informed about health issues.

5. *Children.* To help their children is another important reason that adults give for taking part in ICT learning. Without the required skills parents will be restricted in the support they can offer their children.

6. *Participation.* E-learning is being rapidly developed and has distinct advantages for individuals. However, a successful e-learner is likely to need to be a confident ICT user with a good range of generic/learning skills.

7. *Society.* ICT is clearly changing and has already changed society. The Government's objectives for e-Government are likely to accelerate the process so that without ICT skills people will have less access to information, services and online communities. The pace of change is accelerating so that the disadvantages that a lack of ICT skills bring are growing.

8. *Stigma.* At the moment there is no particular stigma about being a non-user of ICT. However, with the increasing ubiquitous nature of ICT it is probably inevitable that people who are not able to participate will be identified as different. At the moment a failure to use mobile phones, cash machines and other technology is seen as no more than eccentricity, but difference often leads to stigma.

9. *Education.* ICT is being used increasingly in all areas of education. Without the required ICT skills people will find that some educational opportunities are unavailable to them.

10. *Confidence.* Limited ICT skills are likely to make it increasingly difficult for adults to participate confidently in society if they are unable to use or make sense of the multiple technologies that now impact on everyday life.

It is likely that we are a few years away from a society in which people will have daily difficulties in operating without ICT skills but the trend towards this world is probably accelerating. The inevitability of ICT becoming a fundamental part of people's lives is clear. To avoid the problems that excluding a large part of the population from ICT will produce it is probably sensible to address the problem now. Government and other organisations have already made considerable efforts to encourage people to develop their ICT skills. However, the large group of adults who do not see the relevance of ICT to their lives have not been successfully addressed. The concept of a society where a large proportion of the population is further disadvantaged by a lack of ICT skills cannot be accepted and must be addressed.

Key points – summary

Introduction

1. ICT has and is continuing to make significant changes in all aspects of people's lives.
2. ICT has been designated a skill for life.
3. There are approximately 24 million people without ICT skills compared to 7 million with poor basic skills.
4. People with poor basic skills face many barriers and disadvantages in their lives (e.g. lower incomes and periods of unemployment).
5. The definition of basic ICT is likely to include a mixture of functional, structural and generic skills in the context of hardware and software.

Current position

1. By February 2002, 58 per cent of men and 54 per cent of women had used the Internet.
2. The pattern of access to the Internet is complex and shows that many groups are not willing or able to participate. Access is influenced by income (i.e. more likely with higher incomes), geography (i.e. more people have access in the south east of England) and age (i.e. younger people are more likely to have access).
3. People use the Internet for a variety of purposes but sending e-mail and finding information are the key uses.
4. A large majority of non-users have no interest in using the Internet and appear to be unable to see the relevance of ICT to their lives.

Relationship – ICT with literacy and numeracy

1. There is little current stigma in admitting to having poor ICT skills, while there is considerable stigma in having poor basic skills.
2. Many adults are willing to improve their basic skills if it can be done through, or involving, ICT.
3. ICT can contribute to the development of basic skills through a wide variety of means.
4. ICT has contributed to changing the nature of basic skills (e.g. keyboard literacy and specialist terms).

How do people currently use ICT?

1. Communication technologies are the most widely used at home and work.
2. E-mail and the Internet are increasingly becoming part of people's lives.
3. Communication technologies are new developments to many businesses.
4. Many businesses have benefited from the use of ICT and in some cases have come to rely on it.
5. Businesses require a wide range of ICT skills, covering many different applications.
6. Individuals will need to continuously develop and update their ICT skills and knowledge.
7. People will need a good structural understanding combined with the ability to transfer their learning.

Employment

1. Three quarters of the workforce now use computers as part of their work, while 90 per cent of all jobs by 2010 will need IT skills.
2. Many governments have realised that future prosperity requires a well-educated, flexible workforce that can adapt to change as part of the information or knowledge society. The impact that ICT has on the economy of Great Britain and the world is immense.
3. Employers are expected to need people with technical and user ICT skills over the next few years. ICT is an essential component in many jobs and organisations and its influence continues to grow.
4. There is a major shortage of ICT professionals in Europe. The key issue now is not so much the quantity of ICT professionals but rather the quality of skills they can provide.

5. There are approximately one million ICT professionals in Great Britain and their numbers have grown far more rapidly than the rest of the workforce (Institute for Employment Studies, 2001).

6. ICT is altering the nature of work and in particular the location (e.g. teleworking, hot-desking and mobile working).

7. The use of online information is changing the structure of organisations. In some cases traditional hierarchies are no longer necessary.

8. Access to the Internet is now available to the majority of SMEs and a large majority of larger enterprises.

9. About a third of small organisations are not convinced that the Internet is relevant to them. This compares to a similar proportion of individuals.

e-UK

1. Government has already been changed by ICT in similar ways to many other organisations (e.g. working practices).

2. The Government is seeking to make access to itself and its processes more open through ICT.

3. The Government has set a series of objectives for the use of ICT to ensure that Great Britain and its people gain the maximum benefits from the digital world.

4. The possibilities that ICT brings to democracy have been extensively debated (e.g. electronic voting, e-mailing MPs and Local Counsellors or accessing public information) and are emerging.

5. E-mail is emerging as a significant means of communication between citizens and their representatives.

6. The use of online communication to support campaigning is still minor.

e-Learning

1. There is enormous interest in employing ICT to support and deliver learning. Many universities, colleges, Learndirect, training providers and adult education providers are making significant progress in using e-learning.

2. E-learning represents only a small proportion of the total learning opportunities provided for adults but is growing rapidly.

3. E-learning has been identified as having the potential to motivate learners, remove some of the barriers socially disadvantaged adults face and deliver learning.

4. Although ICT skills and knowledge are important for taking part in e-learning or ILT, learners also need a range of more generic skills to be effective (e.g. learning skills).

Everyday life

1. ICT has and is changing the way we live our lives. This is probably accelerating.
2. Online communication is a powerful means of developing social relationships but is not as effective as face-to-face or telephone communications.
3. Almost half of the population regard ICT as being very important to their lives while a large majority of parents believe that computer skills were essential for their children.
4. Attitudes to computers depend on age, class and income of the individual.
5. Online sites offering information on health are amongst the most popular accessed by users.
6. A quarter of the population have bought goods over the Internet (MORI, 2001). The US Department of Commerce reported that online retail shopping increased by 19 per cent from 2000 to 2001.
7. ICT offers the opportunity to allow many people who produce original writings, artwork or other form of self expression to have them published.
8. The Internet now plays a major part in providing information for people's lives (e.g. timetables, traffic news, places to visit, maps, hotels and many other types of information).
9. Online- and ICT-based entertainment is expanding rapidly.
10. It is almost impossible to live in Great Britain and not come into contact with computer technology.
11. People are concerned with keeping up with the ICT pace of change.

Digital divide

1. ICT has the potential to contribute towards overcoming social exclusion.
2. Socially disadvantaged people often do not have access to technology, are unaware of its benefits to them and are not skilled in its use.
3. Ownership of ICT is skewed by gender, income, age and educational attainment.
4. Public access to ICT is critical for many socially and economically disadvantaged people.
5. This large and continuing growth in public access is only useful if adults are confident and competent users of ICT.
6. National initiatives have proved effective in encouraging people to learn about ICT.

Community

1. ICT can be a powerful influence on community development by being a catalyst for change.
2. Communication technologies can provide a new form of community (e.g. communities of interest). Online communities are not limited by geography or time.
3. People are socially equal online and can present themselves in any way they want.

Defining ICT skills

1. Basic ICT skills need to be defined in terms of functional, structural and generic skills.
2. Existing ICT standards partially meet the needs of basic ICT.
3. ICT entry level standards will be needed.

References

BBC (1999) *Bridging the Digital Divide*, Information Rich, Information Poor, special report. See: http://www.bbc.co.uk/hi/english/special_report/1999/10/99/information_rich_information_poor/466651.stm

Bynner J (2001) *Learning Leads to Better Lives*, press release. See: http://www.ioe.ac.uk/media/r00010703.htm

The Centre for Democracy and Technology (2001) *Bridging the Digital Divide: Internet Access in Central and Eastern Europe*. Washington DC: The Centre for Democracy and Technology. At: http://www.cdt.org/international/ceeaccess/eereport.pdf

Clarke A (1998) *IT Awareness Raising for Adults*. London: Department of Education and Employment, OL 254.

Clarke A (1999) *How to Create Effective Information and Communication Technology Learning Programmes*. Leicester: NIACE.

Clarke A (2002a) *Online Learning Skills*. Leicester: NIACE.

Clarke A (2002b) *Online Learning and Social Exclusion*. Leicester: NIACE.

Clarke A (2002c) *New CLAIT Student Workbook*. London: Hodder and Stoughton Educational.

Coleman S and Normann, E (2000) *New Media and Social Inclusion*, Hansard E-Democracy Programme. London: Hansard Society.

Crowston K and Sawyer S (2000) How do information and communication technologies reshape work? Evidence from the residential real estate industry. In: *Proceedings of the Twenty-first International Conference on Information Systems, Brisbane, Australia*. Atlanta, GA, USA: Association for Information Systems.

Cummings JN, Butler B and Kraut R (2002) The quality of online social relations. *Communications of the ACM* 45(7): 103–108.

Cybrarian Project (2002) At: http://www.dfes.uk/elearningstrategy
DELG (2002) *Report of the LSC's Distributed and Electronic Learning Group.* At: http://www.lsc.gov.uk/news_docs/DELG_REPO627.doc

Department for Education and Skills (2001) *Employer Skill Survey.* At: http://www.skillsbase.dfes.gov.uk/narrative/narrative.asp?Sect=7

Department for Education and Skills (2001) *ICT Access and Use: Report on the Benchmark Survey*, Research Report 252. London: DfES.

Department for Education and Skills (2002) *Success For All: Reforming Education and Training.* Consultation document on the future of further education and training. London: DfES.

Department for Education and Skills (2003a) *21st Century Skills: Realising Our Potential.* London: DfES.

Department for Education and Skills (2003b) *Towards a Unified e-Learning Strategy*, consultation document. London: DfES.

Department of Trade and Industry (1996) *IT For All: A Survey Into Public Awareness of, Attitudes Towards, and Access to Information and Communication Technologies.* London: DTI.

Department of Trade and Industry (1997) *IT For All: The Latest Findings concerning Attitudes towards IT.* London: DTI.

Department of Trade and Industry (2000a) *Closing the Digital Divide: Information and Communication Technologies in Deprived Areas*, a report by Policy Action Team 15. London: DTI.

Department of Trade and Industry (2000b) *Working Anywhere: Exploring Telework for Individuals and Organisations.* UK Online for business, at: http://www.dti.gov.uk

Ducheneaut N and Bellotti V (2001), E-mail as habitat: an exploration of embedded personal information management. *Interactions* 8(5): 30–38.

e-Envoy (2002) At: http://www.e-envoy.gov.uk/index-content.htm

e-Health (2002) At:
http://europa.eu.int/information_society/eeurope/action_plan/ehealth/index_en.htm

e-Learning Task Force (2002) *Get on With IT*. At:
http://www.dfes.gov.uk/elearningstrategyunit

Electoral Commission (2001)At: http://www.electoralcommission.gov.uk/moripoll

Hansard Society (2002) At: http://www.hansard-society.org.uk/eDemocracy.htm

Healey J (2002) *Greater Investment and Influence for IT Sector*, Department for
Education and Skills Press Release, 29 May 2002. London: DfES.

Hellawell S and Mulquin M (2000) *Putting IT into Practice: New Technology and the
Modernising Agenda*. Soham, Ely: IS Communications Ltd.

Hillage J, Millar J and Willison R (2002) *An Assessment of Skill Needs in Information
and Communication Technology*, DfES Skills Dialogue SD5. London: DfES.

Home Office Partnership (1999) At: http://www.homeoffice.gov.uk

Institute for Employment Studies (2001) *An Assessment of Skill Needs in Information
and Communication Technology*. London: DfES.

Jowell T (2001) *Jowell Calls for European IT Skills Task Force*, D for Education and
Skills Press Release, 15 February 2001. London: DfES.

Learndirect (2002) At: http://www.ufiltd.co.uk/press/facts/default.asp

Learning and Skills Council (2002) *Distributed and Electronic Learning Group Report*.
Coventry: LSC.

Mackay W (1998), More than just a communication system: Diversity in the use of
Electronic Mail. *ACM Transactions on Office Information Systems* 6(4): 380–397.

Measuring Information Society (1997) At:
http://www.europa.eu.int/information_society_en.htm

MORI (2000) *Dotcom Up and See Me Sometime*, report for Motorola. At:
http://www.mori.com/polls/2000/motbandt.shtml

MORI (2001) *Informing Consumers About e-commerce: Quantitative Survey Report*.
London: Department for Trade and Industry.

Moser C (1999) *Improving Literacy and Numeracy: A Fresh Start*. A report of the working group chaired by Sir Claus Moser. London: Department for Education and Skills.

National Statistics (2000) At: http://www.statistics.gov.uk

National Statistics (2001) *Census 2001*. At: http://www.statistics.gov.uk/census2001

National Statistics (2002) At: http://www.statistics.gov.uk

National Strategy (2001) *Skills for Life: The National Strategy for Improving Adult Literacy and Numeracy Skills*. London: Department for Education and Skills.

Neighbourhood Renewal Unit (2001) *Skills and Knowledge Programme*. London: Department of the Environment, Transport and the Regions.

NHS (1998) *Information for Health: An Information Strategy for the Modern NHS 1998–2005. A National Strategy for Local Implementation*. London: NHS Executive.

OCR (2002a) *OCR Level 1 Certificate for IT Users (New CLAIT)*. At: http://www.ocr.org.uk

OCR (2002b) *OCR Level 2 Certificate for IT Users (CLAIT Plus)*. At: http://www.ocr.org.uk

OECD (1997) *Literacy Skills for the Knowledge Society*. Ottawa, Ontario, Canada: Human Resource Development Canada.

OECD (2002) *OECD Information Technology Outlook Highlights*. Paris: Organisation for Economic Co-operation and Development.

Office of the Deputy Prime Minister (2002) At: http://www.local-regions.odpm.gov.uk/egov/index.htm

Oftel (2001) *Small and Medium Business Survey Wave 5*, May/June 2001. London: Oftel.

Open University (2002) At: http://www3.open.ac.uk/media/factsheets/index.asp

Parity (2002) *MPs Just Want to be Faxed*. News archive, 15 August 2002. At: http://www.parity.net

Pettigrew M and Elliott D (1999) *Student IT Skills*. Aldershot: Gower Publishing Ltd.

Preece J (2001) *Online Communities*. New York: Wiley.

QCA (2002) At: http://www.qca.org.uk

Raynsford N (2002) *National Strategy Consultation*. At:
http://www.press.dtlr.gov.uk/egov/index.htm

Rutland Business Survey (2000) At: htttp://www.rutnet.co.uk/rcc/ictsurvey

Shearman C (1999) *Local Connections: Making the Net Work for Neighbourhood Renewal*. London: Communities Online.

Slyke CV, Comunale CL and Belanger F (2002) Gender differences in perceptions of web-based shopping. *Communications of the ACM* **45**(8): 82–86.

Social Exclusion Unit (2000) *National Strategy for Neighbourhood Renewal, Report of Policy Action Team 16: Learning Lessons*. London: Stationery Office Books.

Taylor C (2002) *Workshop Laptop Initiative*. London.

The Learning and Business Link Company (2001) *ICT in the New Economy*, LBL theme papers, No. 1: Kent and Medway Learning and Skills Council. Kent: The Learning and Business Link Company.

US Census Bureau (2001) *Home Computers and Internet Use in the USA in August 2000*. US Department of Commerce.

Wellman B (2001) Physical place and cyberplace: the rise of networked individualism. In: L Keeble and BD Loader (eds) *Community Informatics: Shaping Computer-Mediated Social Relations*. New York: Routledge.

Williams D, Wilson K, Richardson A, Tuson J and Coles L (1998) *Teachers' ICT Skills and Knowledge Needs: Final Report to SOEID*. Aberdeen, Scotland: School of Information and Media, Faculty of Management, Robert Gordon University. At: http://www.scotland.gov.uk/library/ict/append-title.htm

Useful links/contacts

AbilityNet: http://www.abilitynet.co.uk

Basic Skills Agency: http://www.basic-skills.co.uk

BBC Education: http://www.bbc.co.uk/education

British Association for Open Learning, Pixmore House, Pixmore Avenue, Letchworth, Hertfordshire, SG6 1J6: http://www.baol.co.uk

British Educational Communication Technology Agency (Becta): http://www.becta.org.uk

British Museum: http://www.thebritishmuseum.ac.uk

Capella University: http://www.capellauniversity.edu/gateway.aspx

CCTA: http://www.ccta.gov.uk/services/list/gcatmore.htm

City and Guilds: http://www.city-and-guilds.co.uk

Communities Online: http://www.communities.org.uk/home.htm

Department for Environment, Transport and the Regions: http://www.regeneration.detr.gov.uk/98ild

Department of Education and Skills: http://www.dfes.gov.uk

Department of Trade and Industry: http://www.dti.gov.uk

e-Envoy: http://www.e-envoy.gov.uk

Electoral Commission: http://www.electoralcommission.gov.uk

Employment NTO: http://www.empnto.co.uk

e-Skills NTO: http://www.e-skills.com

Help is at Hand, UK Online Centres support: http://centres.ngfl.gov.uk

House of Commons: http://www.parliament.uk

Learndirect: http://www.ufiltd.co.uk

Learning and Skills Council: http://www.lsc.gov.uk

Learning and Skills Development Agency: 3 Citadel Place, Tinworth Street, London, SE11 5EF, http://www.lsda.org.uk

National Gallery: http://www.nationalgallery.org.uk

National Institute of Adult Continuing Education (NIACE): Renaissance House, 20 Princess Road West, Leicester, LE1 6TP: http://www.niace.org.uk

National Training Organisations National Council: 10 Meadowcourt, Amos Road, Sheffield, S9 1BX: http://www.nto-nc.org

Office of National Statistics: http://www.statistics.gov.uk

Open and Distance Learning Quality Council, 16 Park Crescent, London, WIH 4AH: http://www.odlqc.org.uk

Open University: http://www.open.ac.uk

Organisation of Economic Co-operation and Development: http://www.oecd.org

Oxford, Cambridge and RSA (OCR): http://www.ocr.org.uk

Quality and Curriculum Authority (QCA): http://www.qca.org.uk

Resource (The Council for Museums, Archives and Libraries): http://www.resource.gov.uk

Tate Gallery: http://www.tate.org.uk/home/default.htm

The Telework, Telecottage and Telecentre Association: http://www.tca.org.uk

UK Online Centres: http://www.dfes.gov.uk/ukonlinecentres

Visit Britain, official guide: http://www.visitbritain.com

Workers' Educational Association: http://www.wea.org.uk

OTHER BOOKS AVAILABLE FROM **niace**

Online Learning and Social Exclusion

Alan Clarke

ISBN 1 86201 115 X, 2002, 104pp

Online learning has the potential to overcome the barriers of pace, place and time of learning so as to deliver learning to almost any location with a telephone line. This book considers the nature of the different approaches to online learning in relation to adults who are socially or economically disadvantaged to reveal how this potential can be realised.

Online Learning Skills

Alan Clarke

ISBN 1 86201 152 2, 2002, 48pp

Online learning skills have a relationship with more general study skills, yet there are specific competences that need to be acquired. This practical guide provides ideas and suggestions for practitioners in developing online learning skills with their learners. Written in an open learning style, the guide includes short exercises and discussion sections on themes including self-management, communication, reading and note-taking, self-assessment and learning strategies.

These books can be ordered from NIACE by contacting Publications Sales, NIACE, Renaissance House, 20 Princess Road West, Leicester LE1 6TP
Tel: +44 (0)116 204 4216; Fax: +44 (0)116 204 4276; e-mail: orders@niace.org.uk; Or, order online at **www.niace.org.uk/publications**